SMALLGROUP
ToolBox

HEARING GOD

Ron Kallmier

CONTENTS

PREFACE

Writing this book presented me with a significant personal challenge. On the one hand, it is a topic in which I am extremely interested and one that I have taught in church services and in seminars over a number of decades. There have been times when God has clearly communicated His desires to my wife Jeanette and me. On the other hand, to be totally honest, there have also been those puzzling times when God has appeared silent, even disinterested in my prayers or my needs and in this, I have identified with the writings of many of the psalmists (eg Psa. 10:1; 22:1–2). Yet, despite this mix of experiences the pursuit of God continues to be a central part of my life. I resonate with the ancient words of Richard of Wyche, the Bishop of Chichester (1197–1253) who is quoted as saying:

> Thanks be to thee, my Lord Jesus Christ, for all the benefits Thou hast given me, for all the pains and insults thou hast borne for me. O most merciful redeemer, friend and brother, **may I know thee more clearly, love thee more dearly and follow thee more nearly, day by day.** (emphasis mine)[1]

It is also important that you understand, from the beginning, that I use 'hearing God' in the broadest sense. In this book 'hearing God' describes every way that God chooses to communicate with us.

In preparing my introductory comments for this study book, I spent some time reflecting on the most common ways that I have become aware of God communicating with me over the years. Naturally, the Scriptures have played a significant part – not just the random snatching of verses from here and there but rather those ideas and instructions which the Holy Spirit continues to impress on my mind from time to time. (I cannot over-emphasise how important my knowledge of the Bible text has been in this.) Additionally, I have also been drawn into God's presence through some wonderful experiences in nature that have been awe-inspiring and caused me to respond in praise and worship.

The wise words of people I trust, who have been God's voice to me on many occasions – either prophetically or with wisdom beyond the ordinary – should also be mentioned in this list as should those times when God has clearly opened or closed doors, or challenged Jeanette and me through other means to make a significant change in our life direction. On these occasions there has been a sense of 'rightness', although often accompanied by a feeling of insecurity and uncertainty that has required us to move forward in an act of simple faith in Him. Profound dreams have played their part occasionally and there are also those Christians who have received a gift of wisdom from God, some of them at a very young age.

Finally, I would include personal insights and a wisdom that has grown through my own assessment of my life experiences and through my seeking to understand God's perspective on them. This is one of the benefits of growing older.

While I recognise that my journey will not be the same as yours, I offer this study book in the hope that it will provide you with a number of helpful insights and provocative questions to stimulate your spiritual growth and enrich your small group.

I pray that you will enjoy your journey together as you look further into this vital topic.

Ron Kallmier, 2012

1. Quotation from: http://justus.anglican.org/resources/bio/139.html

SUGGESTIONS FOR USING THIS STUDY GUIDE

SUGGESTIONS FOR GROUP LEADERS

- As far as possible keep discussions practically orientated, including the Bible study section each week.

- Many of the suggestions for individuals and groups are quite 'meaty' and you may find that you only cover one of these during a group session. This is OK.

- Encourage the group members to do some preparation for the following week. Their best preparation may be as simple as thinking over how they respond to the questions or issues featured in each study.

- For many Christians this is both a fascinating and a confusing topic. From our reading of the Bible we know that God can and does speak to individuals, but some of the deeper questions that arise may include:

  'Does He speak to me today?'

  'How can I know when God has spoken to me?'

  'What if I don't hear anything?'

- The group times will be most effective if there is integrity and honesty in the discussion. It is the leader who will be the best example and best encourager in facilitating openness among group participants.

- There are four parts to each of the studies in this book. First, the 'Preview' briefly introduces the set topic and highlights some key Bible verses that help to get readers thinking. Next, 'Personal Exploration' has an individual focus, guiding personal study and reflection. Third, 'Studying Together' provides questions and suggestions for discussing the key Bible passages within a small group context. Finally, 'Applying the Scriptures' raises some thought-provoking questions about practical issues involved in hearing God today.

- Naturally, you are free to use the suggestions in any way that best fits your own group. While the book is designed to be covered in four small-group sessions, you may find it helpful to use some of the suggestions, discard others and add your own too. Feel free to take as many sessions as you believe are necessary to cover this important topic thoroughly.

- It is recommended that you address real questions and real issues from within the group whenever this is appropriate. Sessions are not intended to be merely a theoretical discussion, but should be very practical.

- In a healthy group environment, positive experiences and any uncertainties or concerns of group members will surface. This openness will stimulate frank and open exploration of the issues raised.

- Ideally, group members should complete this study series feeling encouraged and having grown in their confidence to discern God's wisdom and God's ways for themselves.

- By the way, we suggest you don't pressure anyone to be involved in the discussion if they appear unwilling. Make space for individuals to process their own thoughts and to consider what is being said by others.

SUGGESTIONS FOR YOUR PERSONAL USE

- This study series aims to apply biblical experiences and teaching to the everyday life experiences of individual Christians.

- In addition to the spaces provided in this study book, you may find it useful to get hold of a small journal or note book to use while you are focusing on this topic. Here are some things you may like to jot down:

  - Some key times when you have been aware of God's words or God's wisdom or God's provision coming to you.
  - Any reliable experiences of Christians you know or have read about who have heard from God.
  - Any confusion you may have or questions that you want to bring before God in prayer or to your group if you are part of one.

SUGGESTIONS FOR SMALL GROUPS

- If you plan to use the book in a small group, it is recommended that group members all read the 'Preview' section and spend some time in personal preparation for the next group meeting. With our busy lives, this may be quite a challenge but the preparation will help to give maximum benefit to all group members.

- Usually group members find themselves in very different places spiritually when this topic is raised. It is also a topic where individual Christians may hold quite diverse views because of their background and personal experiences, so it is important that everyone is respectfully heard and understood. Each person's perspective should be appreciated, even when it is not that of other people in the group.

- We can all learn from one another, even from those of us who have serious doubts or questions. Of course, we will need to turn to the Scriptures as our primary authority and source for exploring the history of God's communication with His people over the centuries.

INTRODUCTION

THE PURSUIT OF GOD

To hear regularly from God requires a deep desire and the orientation of our whole being towards Him and His purposes. This is not a casual quest. As the writer of the letter to the Hebrews puts it: 'And without faith it is impossible to please God, because anyone who comes to him must believe that he exists and that he rewards those who earnestly seek him' (Heb. 11:6).

Whatever approach we take in our efforts to discern the voice of God, the most important thing is to have, as our top priority, a mind that desires to go after God. **Attitude and awareness** are more important than **activity** in achieving this. As the psalmist encourages us, 'Trust in the LORD and do good; dwell in the land and enjoy safe pasture. Delight yourself in the LORD and he will give you the desires of your heart. Commit your way to the LORD; trust in him and he will do this' (Psa. 37:3–5).

Every one of us is different in the way that we approach God and spend time in His presence. We need to be ourselves and not bound by the rules of others who may have different gifts to ours or who are 'hard-wired' to a certain set of spiritual disciplines. Many sincere Christians have been put off their personal pursuit of God because some well-meaning person has told them that they should do it a certain way (that individual's own way). Of course we **can** learn from the experience of Christians who have gone ahead of us, but each of our journeys will be unique to a greater or lesser degree so we should not feel obliged to copy everything that others do.

Instead, we should begin with whatever works for us – stillness, music, Bible-reading, artistic activity, walking, observing etc. The potential ways of 'being with God' are endless. And let's not think we have to be in some religious pose or activity for God to speak to us. For me, one of the times when God communicated with me most directly and clearly was when I was mowing a large overgrown section of grass on a very hot summer's day. This simple encounter changed the direction of life for Jeanette and me.

FREEDOM OF CHOICE

A clarification is appropriate at this point. Many of life's choices are left to us, though we should always seek God's leading and wisdom in all our daily living. God created us with the power of choice. This was one aspect of His design of human beings, so we are free to make many of life's choices. Our Lord Jesus Christ gave two boundaries within which our choices should operate: **loving God; loving others**. When no clear direction is given to us from God and we must make a decision, we should weigh up the alternatives prayerfully and perhaps seek advice from those in whom we have confidence. We then commit our ways to Him, simply trusting that He will guide us as we make our decisions. God does not desire robots; He created human beings with whom He could interact and relate. Sometimes the struggles and the uncertainties that we face as we make important decisions are the very things God uses to draw our attention back to Himself and our dependency on Him.

GOD OF COMMUNICATION

When we were living in Farnham, Surrey (UK), I remember once driving along one of the roads in autumn. The colour of the trees was stunning, so I stopped to take some photos, and a local man asked me why I was taking them. I told him it was because it looked so beautiful. He gave the scene a cursory glance before replying, 'Yes, I suppose it is'. He returned immediately to his chores without giving the beauty a second glance. It was simply too familiar for him to notice. The apostle Paul, in Romans 1:20, declared that God's divine nature and His eternal power are plain to see in what He has created. To look intently helps us to see something of the greatness of God but, like the man in Farnham, we can miss it if we lack focus. The psalmists understood this. Consider, for example the appreciation of creation in Psalm 8 and 19:1–6.

God's creativity flows into His communication also. He is not limited to an audible voice (physical hearing). Notice the variety of means of communication that God used in biblical history. (See the Appendix.) In addition, we have the wealth of God's communication to us in the whole of Scripture.

For example, when we consider Elijah's experience in 1 Kings 19:9–18, we are reminded that when God communicates with us, His children, it may be intimate and gentle rather than distant, judgmental and demanding as some expect. Being tuned for the still small voice is more demanding than becoming aware of an earthquake, a raging gale or a fierce fire.

His approach to us is based entirely upon His grace and our forgiveness through Jesus Christ. Remember, He remains loving in His attitude towards us, His children, though He will not hesitate to confront us with those things that displease Him. My personal experience suggests that in this process He is **convicting** rather than **condemning**.

GOD IN THE STILLNESS AND SILENCE

Most Christians would say that they do not 'hear' God speak to them in an audible, compelling way on a regular basis, though some do. Sadly, some people who claim to hear from God are mistaken or confused or deluded or deceived.

In the Old Testament we have a record of the occasions when God **did** speak to people; however, those long seasons when they may not have heard from God are not recorded. I believe that even the prophets are unlikely to have received continuous communication from God in the way that many Christians seem to expect. Between the days of Malachi and the birth of Jesus, there was a period of 400 years when no prophetic message was heard.

Nevertheless, the silence of God does **not** mean the absence of God or even the displeasure of God. Since Pentecost we have been promised the comforting, empowering and guiding ministry of the Holy Spirit. Faulty expectations about the reasons for God's apparent lack of communication lead many Christians to judge themselves as being inferior or inadequate or, as being punished for their sins when this is not the case.

MYSTERY

There is a great deal of mystery concerning God's communication with His children. There are no neat boxes here, or 'five easy steps' that will guarantee that He must speak clearly to us. It is in His time and His way. If God was always predictable and we were able to understand Him totally, we would not be in touch with the God of the Bible. He is King of kings yet, in Jesus, He takes on the form of a suffering servant (Isa. 52:13–15; 53). He is both just and loving; both holy and forgiving. A mystery indeed!

In summary, the truth is God has probably been speaking to us more than we realise. Often the problem lies in the distractions of life, our own sense of inadequacy or our failure to pay sufficient attention. So we need to be attuned to those situations where there is clear leading from the Holy Spirit. His peace and affirmation flow into our hearts as we become more confident of God communicating with us personally.

PART ONE

TUNE INTO
THE HEART OF GOD

 PREVIEW

In the Old Testament, heart and spirit or soul appear to be used almost interchangeably. Essentially the heart refers to the centre of who we are, how we think, what we value, what motivates us, and the state of our spiritual lives. The condition of our hearts is clearly the primary focus of God's attention. Consider the following key passages as we seek to understand God's heart:

> 'Love the LORD your God with all your heart and with all your soul and with all your strength.'
> (Deut. 6:5)

> 'Take heed to yourselves, lest your heart be deceived, and you turn aside and serve other gods and worship them …'
> (Deut. 11:16, NKJV)

> '… he said to them, "Take to heart all the words I have solemnly declared to you this day, so that you may command your children to obey carefully all the words of this law."'
> (Deut. 32:46)

> 'But the LORD said to Samuel, "Do not consider his appearance or his height, for I have rejected him. The LORD does not look at the things man looks at. Man looks at the outward appearance, but the LORD looks at the heart."'
> (1 Sam. 16:7)

'Above all else, guard your heart, for it affects everything you do.'
(Prov. 4:23, NLT)

In His ministry, Jesus picked up the same theme. What is on God's heart needs to be the focus of our hearts too:

'Blessed are the pure in heart, for they will see God.'
(Matt. 5:8)

'Wherever your treasure is, there your heart and thoughts will also be.'
(Matt. 6:21, NLT)

'A good person produces good deeds from a good heart, and an evil person produces evil deeds from an evil heart. Whatever is in your heart determines what you say.'
(Luke 6:45, NLT)

PERSONAL EXPLORATION

1. Psalm 46:10
   What activities help you to be still in God's presence?

   _____

   _____

   _____

   _____

   _____

2. Psalm 37:3–5; Matthew 6:25–34
   How can you separate your wants from your deepest desires – those longings that are in tune with God's purposes for you?

   _____

   _____

   _____

   _____

   _____

3. Psalm 19:1–6

Why not take some quality time to observe or listen to something beautiful that brings you into a place of wonder about God, as David the psalmist often did? You could choose a scene of natural beauty or an inspiring piece of artwork, a photograph or music. What is striking to you? What thoughts and questions does this experience evoke in you?

_____

_____

_____

_____

4. Proverbs 4:23-27

In what sense are our hearts (the centre of our being) so crucial to the direction that our lives take? How do we go about 'guarding our hearts'?

_____

_____

_____

_____

STUDYING TOGETHER

1. Deuteronomy 6:5; Luke 10:27

Discuss how we can apply this instruction to our 21st century lifestyle.

_____

_____

_____

_____

2. Micah 6:8

What are some of the signs that a person is walking humbly before God today?

_____

_____

_____

_____

3. 1 John 3:1–3

Our views of God influence our ability to discern His voice. If we see Him as harsh or distant we will not attempt to draw close. Here, John makes a powerful and moving declaration concerning the love of God. Why is it important for us to understand that God loves us if we want to hear from Him?

_____

_____

_____

_____

_____

4. Psalm 131

This is a powerful image of coming to a place of stillness before God. In what ways does this analogy of a weaned child speak to us today, as we take time to hear from God?

_____

_____

_____

_____

_____

APPLYING THE SCRIPTURES

1. Matthew 5:1–12

This well-known selection from the Sermon on the Mount describes the blessings that God gives to various individuals. Which is the **most attractive blessing**, and which is the **most challenging blessing** for the people in your group? Why have these blessings been chosen?

_____

_____

_____

_____

2. Matt. 5:13–16
   Explore together how the imagery of salt and light applies to
   Christians like us – especially if we live in very tough personal
   situations at home or at work.

   _____

   _____

   _____

   _____

   _____

3. Is being quiet before God a real challenge to anyone in your group?
   What causes this difficulty? What practical suggestions can you give
   to help one another with this struggle?

   _____

   _____

   _____

   _____

   _____

4. If the group is able and willing, invite members to share about a
   time when they felt particularly able to hear from God. Are there any
   common themes here? If so, discuss these themes together.

   _____

   _____

   _____

   _____

   _____

PART TWO

TUNE INTO THE WAYS AND WORKS OF GOD

PREVIEW

> *"'My thoughts are completely different from yours,' says the Lord. "And my ways are far beyond anything you could imagine. For just as the heavens are higher than the earth, so are my ways higher than your ways and my thoughts higher than your thoughts.'"*
> (Isa. 55:8–9, NLT)

How can we know and serve a God so great, so superior in every way to us? I believe that there are guidelines we can uncover in the ministry of Jesus. He took time alone to be with His Father. Clearly He asked His Father what He was doing and how He (Jesus) should participate in this work. This is a good starting point for us too.

For many years I have been fascinated and challenged by a number of standout statements that Jesus made concerning how He kept in tune with the heart and will of His heavenly Father. These statements are recorded in John's Gospel.

> *Jesus gave them this answer: "I tell you the truth, the Son can do nothing by himself;* **he can do only what he sees his Father doing, because whatever the Father does the Son also does."**
> (John 5:19, emphasis mine)

'By myself I can do nothing; I judge only as I hear, and my judgment is just, for I seek not to please myself but him who sent me.'
(John 5:30, emphases mine)

'For I did not speak of my own accord, but the Father who sent me commanded me what to say and how to say it. I know that his command leads to eternal life. So whatever I say is just what the Father has told me to say.'
(John 12:49–50, emphases mine)

Hmmm! Here Jesus sets the standard and the challenge for us. So, what is the Father doing in our individual spheres of influence? We need to ask Him to show us how we can participate in His work and then keep our heart and eyes open in order to recognise the opportunities that come our way each day.

PERSONAL EXPLORATION

Perhaps the thought of coming into God's presence produces fear or uncertainty within you. This fear and reluctance will certainly keep you at a 'safe' distance from God, though you are not really distant (see Acts 17:27). For your personal preparation this week, consider the following scriptural passages that challenge any sense of unworthiness:

Zechariah 3:1–10
Luke 5:1–10
James 4:7–10
Isaiah 1:18
Hebrews 4:14–16
2 Kings 6:8–18
Jeremiah 31:3

Why not read them all, asking God to reveal Himself to you as you read? Then, set aside some time before your small group meets again. Go back over any Bible passage(s) that spoke to you, interact with the verse(s) and meditate on their meaning and relevance to you right now. Bring your findings and questions before God in quiet prayer.

Using the space below, or your personal devotional journal, write down your thoughts and record any actions that you plan to fulfil to strengthen your relationship with God in the future.

STUDYING TOGETHER

1. Isaiah 55:6–13

    Though God thinks and acts on a different level to us, what **key words** do you find in these verses that can help us position ourselves to be living in God's purposes?

2. Job 1:1–22; 13:15

    Perhaps more than any other Old Testament character, Job confronted the fact that God works differently from our expectations at times. What do we learn from Job's experience and his response to his trials?

3. Acts 16:1–10

   The apostle Paul had a clear sense of his personal mission from God, yet he still needed God's intervention to bring his own ideas and plans into line with God's ways from time to time. How did God guide Paul and his group in this situation? What do we learn for our own lives from Paul's experience?

4. Luke 2:1–20

   The Christmas story is so familiar that we may miss the amazing and intricate planning of God that underlies it. After further reflection, what is most surprising to you about the way that God sent His Son into the world?

APPLYING THE SCRIPTURES

1. Perhaps some of you have found that there is a clash between God's ways and the lifestyle and values of members of your family or people at work or school. Practically speaking, how can we maintain integrity before both God and these people in our daily lives?

2. What can help us make God-pleasing choices in our daily lives, when these choices may put us at a disadvantage compared with those who are prepared to bend the rules a little or a lot?

3. One of the more positive outcomes of the internet for Christians has been the way that we can access information so quickly about what God is doing in other parts of our country and world. These reports of God at work can be very encouraging. Does anyone in your group have a regular internet site or sites where they keep in touch with Christian ministry in other parts of this country or internationally? In what ways has this been helpful?

4. What has been the most helpful, practical advice you have received about how to tune into the ways and works of God?

PART THREE

TUNE INTO THE VOICE OF GOD

 PREVIEW

One of the most common concerns I have heard voiced by committed followers of Jesus is that they fear getting it wrong. In other words, they lack confidence that they can hear God accurately; they worry that they will do the wrong thing and that this will therefore result in God's displeasure.

But think about this. If you have ever experienced an infant growing up in your family you may recall something that can help us at this point. Suppose that you are present as the toddler attempts to take their first faltering steps. Usually all the adults there will be giving encouragement and praise for those first childish efforts. Wouldn't you be amazed if one of the parents, after watching their child take one or two steps before falling down, responded to the child in a harsh tone, *'Why did you fall down? That is unacceptable! You know how to walk now, so just get on with it and no more falling over!'* I think the other adults present would be shocked.

God is as interested in our first faltering steps in following and listening to Him as He is in the competent Christian walk of the most mature believer.

An integral part then of our spiritual growth as followers of Jesus Christ is becoming more sensitive to the voice of the Good Shepherd (see John 10:7–18). Continuing the analogy of the young child, I have often been impressed by the ability of a mother with a young baby to identify the child's first cries – even in a noisy crowd and with other infants present. How do they do that? I suppose it must come from the many hours that they spend, day and night, tuning their ears to that cry. Hearing God is similar in some ways. With the help of the Holy Spirit, it takes time and serious attention to distinguish His voice.

THE 'VOICES' WE MAY HEAR

Our uncertainty sometimes over what is God's Word to us comes from our awareness that there may be more than one voice speaking into our lives. I have identified four main voices that we can hear.

1. The most common voice we hear originates within our human mind and spirit (heart). A mixture of positive and negative, clear and confusing, uplifting and depressing messages, flow from this source.

2. We are also influenced by the words of other significant persons – past or present – in our lives. The impact of these people may be (or may have been) positive and uplifting or damaging and degrading.

3. The corrupting influence of the enemy of our souls cannot be overlooked (eg Gen. 3:1–19; Matt. 4:1–11).

4. The heart of God gently touching our hearts through His Holy Spirit is the voice that we Christians are most eager to hear.

Sometimes we may be confused by a combination of these 'voices'. So, which should we respond to positively and which should we reject?

'HOW CAN I RECOGNISE THE VOICE OF GOD?'

There is no single correct answer to this question. When I have been seeking to discern the voice of God, I have asked myself the following questions. Perhaps you may also find them helpful.

- **Does this 'voice' I hear promote fear, guilt or selfishness in me?**
  If so, it is most probably not a word from God.

- **Does it require a degree of faith on my part?** Often godly visions require considerable faith to simply believe that we have heard His voice and then to trust in His guidance and His provision as we respond.

- **Will it bring glory to God and/or extend His kingdom?**

- **Is it simple or complicated?** Historically, God has been quite clear in His instructions to His servants. This does not mean that His

25

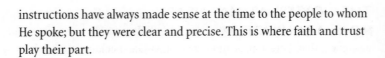

instructions have always made sense at the time to the people to whom He spoke; but they were clear and precise. This is where faith and trust play their part.

- **Is there any other external support for accepting this as accurate?** Are other mature Christians whom I trust in agreement with me on it?

- **Do alternative options not sit well with me?** This is particularly helpful when a choice has to be made from more than one option.

- **Has there been any prophetic confirmation?** There have been times when what was brewing in my heart has been confirmed by prophetic or prayerful people who either did not know me or did not know what was going on inside me. This confirmation has come face to face or by letter or email.

- **Is there a relevant passage of Scripture that keeps coming to mind when I think about this?** The Holy Spirit may persistently focus our attention on one verse or a selection from Scripture that is pertinent to the situation.

- **Do I recognise the peace of God in my heart as I consider this particular option?** For me, this has been a very important test. I prefer not to make a decision when confusion is rife within me. The words of Philippians 4:6–8 have provided essential wisdom along the way:

> *'**Don't worry about anything**; instead, **pray about everything**. Tell God what you need, and thank him for all he has done. If you do this, you will experience God's peace, which is far more wonderful than the human mind can understand. **His peace will guard your hearts and minds as you live in Christ Jesus**. And now, dear friends, let me say one more thing as I close this letter. **Fix your thoughts on what is true and honourable and right**. Think about things that are pure and lovely and admirable. Think about things that are excellent and worthy of praise.'*
> (NLT, emphases mine)

'HOW CAN WE HEAR GOD MORE CLEARLY AND MORE ACCURATELY?'

Through my own experiences, I have compiled the following list of suggestions which I hope may provide some practical suggestions for tuning into God more effectively.

- Over the centuries, Christians who have walked closely with God have spent time reading and meditating on the Bible. Of course not everyone has a Bible today and not everyone enjoys reading – many Christians now listen to the Scriptures or watch dramatised versions of Bible stories on DVDs or the internet. Nevertheless, it's important to remember that the more familiar with the Bible we become, the more the Holy Spirit is able to pour His light upon key verses or passages at appropriate times.

- We need to become sufficiently aware of the content of the Gospels in particular, so that we become familiar with the heart of Jesus Christ, the Good Shepherd. Ask yourself: What do the Gospel accounts teach me about the heart of Jesus?

- We will benefit from increasing our understanding of the amazing grace in which we live through Jesus Christ. This produces great boldness and confidence which can help us overcome any fear of disapproval or rejection by God.

- Like Solomon many years ago, we should persist in asking God for wisdom for both the trivial and the trying situations of our lives.

- A high priority should be to set our hearts to do whatever God tells us. His way is always best and He is able to do more than we can ask or imagine (Eph. 3:20–21).

- Let's learn from our past successes and failures and let's not waste our mistakes.

A FINAL CLARIFICATION

A number of Christians who have talked to me over the years have expected God to speak to them so clearly and precisely with His instructions that they would never make a mistake. This has not been my personal experience and, on reflection, I think this approach misses the point. Certainly a boss may act that way, or a sports coach, perhaps even a caring parent at times, but God invites us into a 'friendship relationship' with Him, and true friendship does not operate this way. The communication in a deep friendship is often far more subtle and may even occur without words. Perhaps it would help us to hear God more effectively if we were to come to Him **as our friend**, just as Moses did:

> '*The Lord would speak to Moses face to face, as a man speaks with his friend.*'
> (Exod. 33:11)

> (See also 2 Chron. 20:7; Prov. 18:24; Luke 7:34; John 15:14.)

To develop the level of intimacy that comes from being known as 'a friend of God', we must begin with a humble recognition of His surpassing greatness, glory and power. This humility is founded on our recognition that God is our Creator and that our position is as His creature. Clearly, reaching this level of understanding and intimacy of friendship is not a casual process; it takes time, dedication and a re-alignment of our life priorities – as we observe in the words of the psalmist:

> '*I have sought your face with all my heart; be gracious to me according to your promise.*'
> (Psa. 119:58)

PERSONAL EXPLORATION

1. Can you identify a time when you were acutely aware of the voice of God in your life? What was the context? What was the result of your response to God? What did you learn from that experience?

2. Turn to the Appendix at the end of this book. Have you sensed that God has communicated with you in ways like any of the biblical examples recorded there?

3. Many Christians find that the Holy Spirit speaks to them out of the Scriptures. What has been your experience in this? What gives you confidence that a particular passage may have relevance for you today and not only for the people to whom it was originally written?

4. John 10:7–18

   Read this passage through thoughtfully. You may find it helpful to turn the teaching of Jesus into a personal prayer. For example, when you read that Jesus said, 'My sheep hear my voice,' you could pray something like, 'Lord help me to hear Your voice more clearly'.

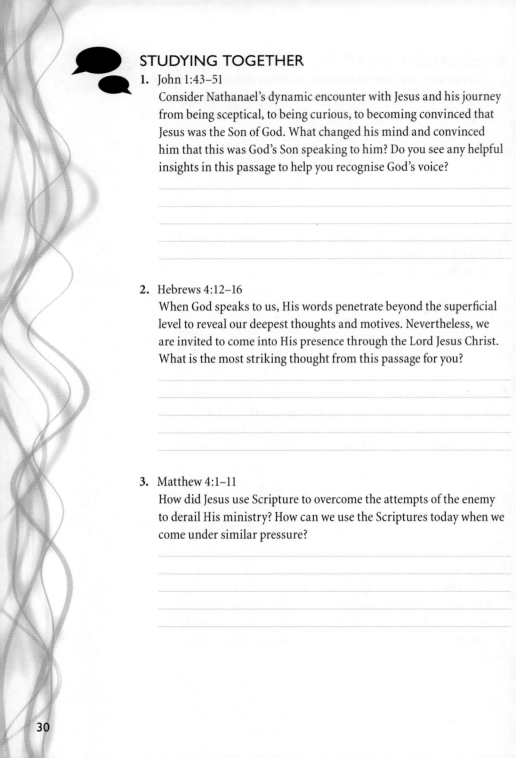

STUDYING TOGETHER

1. John 1:43–51

   Consider Nathanael's dynamic encounter with Jesus and his journey from being sceptical, to being curious, to becoming convinced that Jesus was the Son of God. What changed his mind and convinced him that this was God's Son speaking to him? Do you see any helpful insights in this passage to help you recognise God's voice?

2. Hebrews 4:12–16

   When God speaks to us, His words penetrate beyond the superficial level to reveal our deepest thoughts and motives. Nevertheless, we are invited to come into His presence through the Lord Jesus Christ. What is the most striking thought from this passage for you?

3. Matthew 4:1–11

   How did Jesus use Scripture to overcome the attempts of the enemy to derail His ministry? How can we use the Scriptures today when we come under similar pressure?

4. Acts 10:1–20

There are occasions when God chooses to use more unusual means to communicate with His servants. In this episode in the life of the apostle Peter, we learn of angelic visitations and visions. Why did God choose to communicate in this way in this situation?

APPLYING THE SCRIPTURES

1. Matthew 6:25–34; 11:28–30

The words of Jesus carry the divine weight of heaven with them and are just as appropriate for us today. Consider the relevance of these statements from Matthew's Gospel for people in your group.

2. Has anyone in the group had precise leading from the Scriptures that became the personal voice of God to them in a particular situation?

3. Open up a time for discussion. Are there any further questions that individuals want to raise on this issue of hearing God's voice today?

4. Give an opportunity for group members to share their personal experiences of identifying God's voice in their lives, or in the lives of people whom they know.

PART FOUR

TUNE INTO THE WISDOM OF GOD

PREVIEW

If you could make one request of God and be absolutely sure that He would grant your request, what would you ask for? This was the experience of King Solomon, recorded in the Old Testament:

'That night God appeared to Solomon and said, "What do you want? Ask, and I will give it to you!"' (2 Chron. 1:7, NLT).

This was not a trick but rather a test which forced Solomon to search his own heart and reveal it before God. With all the possibilities open to him and, knowing what other kings would have asked for, it is amazing that Solomon asked God for the wisdom and knowledge to fulfil his role as king over God's people. So pleased was God with Solomon's answer that He promised that Solomon would not only receive so much wisdom and knowledge that he would astound others, but that he would also surpass other kings in every possible way – in wealth, riches and fame.

The Book of Proverbs has many examples of Solomon's wisdom that still resonate with God's people today. It is quite clear from Proverbs that Solomon understood that wisdom must be desired and pursued.

We need look no further than the encounters of Jesus, particularly with the hostile religious leaders, to clarify what godly wisdom looks like. Matthew 22:15–22 is, for me, one of the most stunning examples. Should the Jews pay taxes to Caesar or should they not? The trap is set. If Jesus supports paying taxes the religious leaders will accuse Him of being a Roman sympathiser. If He says they should **not** pay taxes, they will report Him to the Roman authorities. A perfect plan. Well, not quite. The wisdom of God provided not only a way out of the trap but in fact,

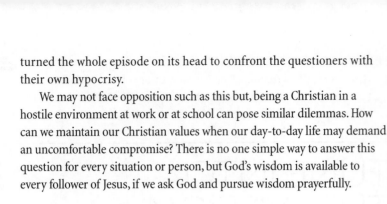

turned the whole episode on its head to confront the questioners with their own hypocrisy.

We may not face opposition such as this but, being a Christian in a hostile environment at work or at school can pose similar dilemmas. How can we maintain our Christian values when our day-to-day life may demand an uncomfortable compromise? There is no one simple way to answer this question for every situation or person, but God's wisdom is available to every follower of Jesus, if we ask God and pursue wisdom prayerfully.

WISDOM AND KNOWLEDGE

Knowledge can be accumulated from our own observations, our study, our experiences, or directly from God Himself. Regrettably we may find that for many people, their knowledge gives them a sense of pride and superiority. As Paul says in 1 Corinthians 8:1, 'Knowledge puffs up, but love builds up'. For a healthy balance, knowledge must be partnered with wisdom.

Wisdom shows us how to use knowledge astutely. Wisdom provides us with the insights to act in the most appropriate way in a particular situation. Sometimes we only recognise with hindsight that God's wisdom has been at work in our lives.

Whilst there are many wise people in the world, there are many times when the wisdom and knowledge from God surpass the limits of our education, our knowledge and our experience. As an example, consider Peter and John in Acts 4:1–22 when they are brought before the Sanhedrin supreme court.

As the Scriptures teach us, God is the ultimate source of all true wisdom. Biblical wisdom addresses the big picture, the longer consequences of actions, and pursues the best outcomes. This breadth of understanding is not available to human beings from within themselves. Despite their limitations, a truly wise person is one who seeks to honour and please God in every aspect of their life.

PERSONAL EXPLORATION

1. Can you recall a situation when you were aware of God's wisdom being given to you when you were in great need of it? What were the most important things that you learned from that experience?

2. James 1:5
   Is there a situation that you are in right now that requires more wisdom than you have? Reconsider the encouragement given by James and use it as a basis for prayer about the dilemma you are facing.

3. Psalm 8
   The seeking of godly wisdom starts with our recognition of how great God is. Spend time in meditating on Psalm 8 as you join in the wonder of the psalmist at God's majesty and His care for us.

4. 1 Corinthians 1:18–25
   If you are one of the many Christians who feel inferior because of your background or abilities, consider this passage and begin to understand that God is not limited by your limitations. (We will look at this passage in the small group too.)

STUDYING TOGETHER

1. Proverbs 1:1–7
   Review this key passage on the nature and value of wisdom.
   What stands out to you as you read?

   _____

   _____

   _____

   _____

2. James 1:5–8
   This is a great passage of encouragement. What keys do we find
   concerning wisdom here?

   _____

   _____

   _____

   _____

3. 1 Corinthians 1:18–25
   According to the apostle Paul, what is the difference between worldly
   wisdom and godly wisdom?

   _____

   _____

   _____

   _____

   Matthew 7:24–29
   What was it about the two builders that made one wise and the other
   foolish? What advice can we find in this parable that is relevant to
   our lives as followers of Jesus Christ?

   _____

   _____

   _____

   _____

APPLYING THE SCRIPTURES

1. The Bible has been an essential source of wisdom for Christians since its early times. If they are willing, invite group members to share how they go about finding wisdom for themselves in the Bible to address the everyday challenges of their lives.

2. What qualities would you expect to find in a person who is wise in the ways of God? Have you known any individual(s) who fit this description?

3. From your experience, what part have trusted Christian friends played in giving you the wisdom you needed during testing times?

4. Are any of the group members facing situations right now that require greater wisdom than they possess? After they have described their situation, why not spend time in prayer asking God to intervene on their behalf and provide the wisdom they require.

FINDING OUR WAY WHEN THINGS ARE UNCLEAR

From my own experience and the experience of people I know, I have identified four main things that may help us:

- We should not be paralysed by the fear of possible mistakes. God has promised to guide us if we are taking the wrong path, provided our hearts are set on seeking to do His will (see Isaiah 30:19–21). It is equally important that we should not be immobilised by the fear of displeasing God. Remember that He has given us the gift of choice. There are many times when the decision on what to do is up to us.

- We grow through constructive self-evaluation when we are willing to review the consequences of our important choices. We do this by asking ourselves, 'What was the outcome of my action or choice? Was it a positive outcome?' If it did not work out as we expected, we can learn from the experience. Remember that God is interested in our **heart** pleasing Him.

- Let's reflect and give thanks when the Lord's guidance is clear. How did we receive that wisdom? What can we learn from that experience for the future? Let's be thankful to God also when our decisions produce positive results for ourselves and for others.

- Our Christian life was never meant to be lived out alone. It is encouraging for us, and for others we know, when we share our experiences of hearing God's voice. Together we can learn from our successes and failures.

APPROACHING THE BIBLE WISELY – A VITAL MATTER

- As we have noted already, it is important to approach Scripture with a view to learning how to live in a God-pleasing way rather than simply to learn more facts. Taking this approach means we will be able to return to the Scriptures over and over again and receive new insights that are relevant for each unique day and every personal situation.

- To learn from God through the Scriptures it is wise to invite the Holy Spirit to be our Teacher. Keeping notes or a journal can be a very helpful reminder of what God has already done. Journaling not only provides us with a record of our life journey but it also helps us to remember how God has worked to bring us through challenging circumstances. How regularly in the Old Testament period did God command Israel to **remember** what He had done for them? Recalling God's involvement in our past gives us the courage and confidence we need to press ahead into the challenges of the future.

- Sometimes, Christians turn to the Scriptures hoping to find a simple unchanging blueprint for discovering God's will for them. Sadly this is not the intent of the Scriptures. Other people have simply taken a verse or passage out of context and as a result gone astray. The Bible gives us glimpses of God's involvement in the lives of very different people. For us, too, life is constantly changing. We are changing personally. Our world is changing. Our situations are changing. We need to know how to respond in our **current** time period.

- James 1:22–27 leaves us in no doubt about how we should use the Scriptures – not as a way of accumulating head knowledge but as a basis for life application. Summing up, we should avoid being reckless, but, on the other hand, we should not be afraid to make decisions after seeking God's wisdom.

- Taking a 'life application' approach to the Scriptures can be transforming for us as Christians. We may begin with faltering steps in our discernment yet our confidence will grow as we begin to see God's wisdom directing us in the choices we make – whether it be in our homes, our relationships, our workplace or our church life.

- Many Christians have learned to become more sensitive to the quiet prompting of the Holy Spirit. His gentle wisdom may come subtly as a sense of caution in our hearts and minds when we are heading in a wrong direction or as an experience of inner peace when we are heading in a positive direction.

FINAL COMMENTS

Whatever approach we take in the process of hearing the voice of God, the most important thing is to have in our hearts the desire to seek God for Himself as the top priority of our lives. **Awareness** is more important than **activity** in achieving this. This means that learning to become still within ourselves and to recognise His presence in everyday life events (certainly, quite a challenge for busy 21st-century people like ourselves!) can be the most helpful approach we can take.

Ultimately, what matters most is that we seek to be attuned to those situations where there is clear leading from the Holy Spirit. His peace and affirmation are most encouraging at those times when we recognise that God is saying to us, *'This is the way you should go'* (Isa. 30:21, NLT).

APPENDIX: THE GOD OF COMMUNICATION

SOME WAYS THROUGH WHICH GOD COMMUNICATED IN OLD TESTAMENT TIMES

- Acted parables: Jeremiah (Jer. 18:1–10); Ezekiel (Ezek. 4–5)
- Audible voice: Balaam's donkey (Num. 22:21–41); Samuel (1 Sam. 3:1–21); Moses and the burning bush (Exod. 3:1–15)
- Covenants, commandments and promises: Moses (Exod. 20–24)
- Creation: Psalm 19:1–6; Psalm 8
- Dreams and visions: large statue (Dan. 2:31–45); four beasts (Dan. 7:1–28)
- Miraculous signs and wonders: Elijah on Carmel (1 Kings 18:16–39); Gideon's fleece (Judg. 6:36–40)
- Prophets: Hebrews 1:1; 2 Peter 1:19–21
- The Scriptures: Josiah and the scroll in the repaired Temple (2 Kings 22–23)
- Wisdom of others: Jethro and Moses (Exod. 17)
- World events: Micaiah and Ahab (1 Kings 22); Babylonian captivity (Dan. 9:1–19)

SOME WAYS THROUGH WHICH GOD COMMUNICATED IN NEW TESTAMENT TIMES

- Audible voice: Saul and Ananias (Acts 9:10–16)
- Divine discernment: Peter and Simon the sorcerer (Acts 8:18–23)
- Dreams, visions and angels: Joseph (Matt. 1:20–21; 2:19–20); Peter and Cornelius (Acts 10:1–23); Paul (Acts 16:6–10)
- Jesus' parables: the Sower; Wheat and the Weeds; Mustard Seed; Hidden Treasure (Matt. 13)
- Jesus' teaching and ministry: Hebrews 1:2
- Miraculous signs and wonders: Ananias and Sapphira (Acts 5:1–11); Saul, Barnabas and Elymas (Acts 13:4–12)
- Prophets: Acts 13:1–3
- The apostles' teaching: Acts 2:42
- The Holy Spirit within the church community: 1 Corinthians 14
- The Scriptures: 2 Timothy 3:16; 2 Peter 3:14–16

You may like to use these pages to journal your thoughts as you learn to hear from God.

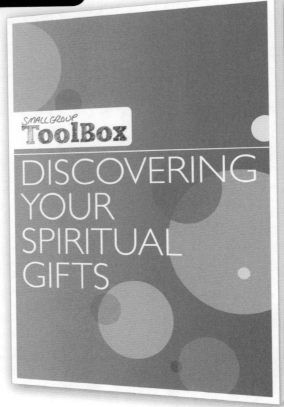

Understand the nature of your spiritual gifts and the reasons why God, in His wisdom, entrusts these to ordinary people.

This resource provides a helpful framework for discovering what the spiritual gifts are, which gifts you may have, and how to use them wisely.

- Ideal for use in small groups
- Helps you find and develop your own unique ministry
- Function in the gifts God has given you

48 pages, paperback, 148x210mm
ISBN: 978-1-85345-765-4

FAITH, HOPE, LOVE AND EVERYTHING IN BETWEEN

Life is a journey not a destination!

Although we don't all travel along the journey of discipleship at the same rate, there is a divine pattern at work which, whilst allowing the widest variety for each person and their own individuality, seeks to bring us closer to God through experiences which are common to us all.

This book will guide you into a deeper understanding of how the Lord will use every person, situation and circumstance in your life to make you more like Jesus.

156 pages, paperback, 153x230mm
ISBN: 978-1-85345-598-8

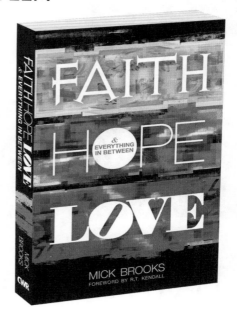

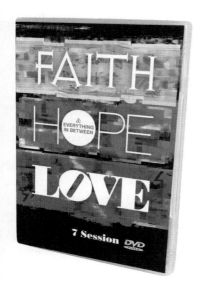

This seven-session DVD provides an honest explanation of the obstacles, opportunities and questions everyone encounters in their spiritual journey of discipleship. The sessions explore how we know God, what it means to be whole and holy and how to:

- Trust God amidst life's ambiguity and mystery
- Gain an eternal perspective
- Develop a closer relationship with God and others

and much more ...

Faith, Hope, Love and Everything in Between DVD
Presented by Mick Brooks
EAN: 5027957001329

For current prices visit www.cwr.org.uk/store
Available online or from Christian bookshops

Transforming lives

CWR's vision is to enable people to experience personal transformation through applying God's Word to their lives and relationships.

Our Bible-based training and resources help people around the world to:
• Grow in their walk with God
• Understand and apply Scripture to their lives
• Resource themselves and their church
• Develop pastoral care and counselling skills
• Train for leadership
• Strengthen relationships, marriage and family life and much more.

Our insightful writers provide daily Bible-reading notes and other resources for all ages, and our experienced course designers and presenters have gained an international reputation for excellence and effectiveness.

CWR's Training and Conference Centre in Surrey, England, provides excellent facilities in an idyllic setting – ideal for both learning and spiritual refreshment.

CWR Applying God's Word
to everyday life and relationships

CWR, Waverley Abbey House,
Waverley Lane, Farnham,
Surrey GU9 8EP, UK

Telephone: **+44 (0)1252 784700**
Email: info@cwr.org.uk
Website: www.cwr.org.uk

Registered Charity No 294387
Company Registration No 1990308